Words of Expression

Words of Expression

Tanya Marie Breaud

ARPress
45 Dan Road Suite 5
Canton MA 02021

Hotline: 1(888) 821-0229
Fax: 1(508) 545-7580

Ordering Information:

Quantity sales. Special discounts are available on quantity purchases by corporations, associations, and others. For details, contact the publisher at the address above.

Printed in the United States of America.

ISBN-13:   Paperback   979-8-89389-535-3
            eBook   979-8-89389-536-0

Library of Congress Control Number: 2024911579

Contents

To all those who have helped to
make this book possible.

Love,

Tanya M. Breaud

Thank You's

I would first like to thank my mother, Jody Breaud, for giving me the strength when I needed it the most. And for always encouraging me to take chances, and for always lending a hand. Thank you, Mom, for giving me so much to cherish for the rest of my life. I love you more than words could ever describe; my heart belongs to you.

And to my sister, Tabitha Breaud, thank you for being my role model, but also a best friend. You always seemed to have found your way to me when I needed you. I'm so grateful to have you. Thank you for being the magnificent and, of course, the most humorous person I have ever known. I love you.

To my brother, Steven Breaud Jr., thank you for making all my bad days become my best. If it wasn't for you, then I swear I'd be miserable. There is never a day when you don't have some- thing smart to say, but I'm glad for that. Thank you for just being there. I love you.

To my beautiful nephew, Trenton Dixon, who became my life the first day you were born. I love you so very much. You're a great inspiration to me and you always will be. Thank the lord and lady for you.

Also, a big thanks to Charles Dixon Jr., for being there to talk to when I had no one. Even though most of the time you didn't really understand me, you still listened. We've had some strange but yet intelligent conversations. Thanks for being there to make me laugh and smile. You're a great friend to have.

To a very good friend of mine, Ka'reem Clark. Thank you for not ever giving up on me, and for not ever walking away from me when I got too confusing to understand. You came into my life with such a content and calm presence. I have always enjoyed your company, listening to what's on your mind. I've gotten some knowledge and great wisdom from you. Thanks for sharing with me what you know, think, feel, and believe. You're an amazing human being, don't ever forget that, and I'll never forget that you were there to encourage me along the way. You have one of the most beautiful hearts.

A special thanks and dedication to Robert Peters. Thanks for being there for me, and for helping out. It means a lot to me to have you in my life. You may not be my blood father, but I'll always remember that it was you helping me practice for all my softball games. I'm glad that it was you and nobody else. It's a good feeling to know that you were willing to accept me as your daughter. Thank you, Bob, I love and miss you.

So many thanks to Tony Rykhus, who made it so hard for me to ever be mad. You brought me great fun and inspiration, maybe for just a short amount of time, but you still put such a big impact in my life. I must say that you are one of the most amazing and most wonderful persons I have been blessed to meet. You'll always have a place in my heart. I love you and miss you.

I would also like to thank Becky (from the UPS store). Thank you for your modesty and kindness. Yeah, everyone learns the hard way. But thanks to you, I made a right move after listening and making a smart choice off your great advice. So much appreciation toward you and your helpful assistance at the UPS store. Thanks again.

Much love and thankfulness goes to Jake Pongratz. I love you more than life itself. The memories I have of you will always be cherished in my heart. For all my hope and love, I thank you.

And last, but not least, thank you to John Beyer, for keeping my butt out of trouble for as long as you did. I appreciated how you looked after me the way you would. Well, guess what? I'm all grown up now-well maybe just a little. To me, you were like, a father figure who would correct me if I was wrong. And now you're in my thoughts every day. Thanks for always listening to me, and for being someone I could run to. Even though I would get annoying at times, you'd still put up with me– thanks. It was a great experience to get to know you. You're in my heart as well, even if you didn't know it before, you do now. Thank you for your unforgettable friendship. I miss you.

I hope I haven't forgotten anyone. It will probably keep me awake and wondering, but hopefully none was forgotten.

Introduction

I've always been told that I feel too much, but I've always believed that feeling too much wasn't enough.

Growing up I've always loved reading poetry, but then after a while I wanted to write it as well. That's when I took up my interest in writing poetry at the age of thirteen. I remember watching my sister create the most beautiful poems in just seconds. She would always tell me that if I don't give it a try, then I'll never know. So, I did, and I couldn't stop writing. It grew to become a big addiction. From what I remember, my family never saw me without paper or pen. Yeah, that was also a habit.

Now, I'd always been the type of person who could never really express myself to others, so I started to find a way through poetry. I find myself always being asked the same question, "Where do I get my inspiration from?" Well, I would have to say "Life," because everything I write has something to do with life's experiences and lessons, and, of course, love, appreciation, hope, and so on.

All the chances I never took, I'm now taking. For the longest time I have searched for a way to express myself. I finally found my way through *Words of Expression*.

Human Nature

Memories begin to take me
on a journey deep within my heart,
but your powerful embrace
brings me back to start.
The human race has always needed
to feel the emotion of love,
 if it can't be felt
then it's sure to be thought of.
I search for unseen secrets to pursue my dreams,
but it's taking forever is what it seems.
My magical spirit is like wildlife
that will continue on,
I'm close to finding
where I belong.
The strongest of all hope will always light the way,
all my wisdom will be known one day.
I tell myself that everyone has their own place,
but I've not yet found my own space.
I'm the living in the race of human nature,
I escape in my dreams because that's my adventure.

Forgive and Forget

It's hard to live your life
when you're being tested every day,
there's no point in cheating
when you're being watched all the way.
Certain emotions are so difficult to feel,
what's the use in pretending when love can be real?
I want everyone to see me for who I am,
I'm not that confusing of a person to understand.
If you listen to my words
and read in between the lines
then you'll see, that I'm taking
this chance to let you get to know me.
The truth will sooner or later unfold,
it should be known no matter how it's told.
Every day I learn so much more,
I now know who I am for sure.
I know that things won't always go my way,
life gets harder every single day.
This time there's no reason for regret,
I would rather forgive and forget.

Nobody Else

It was so easy to fall in love with your heart,
I made a vow and I will not part.
Contacting you with a single smile,
being with you is worth every while.
Proving that my love is real,
I can give you what I feel.
No more emptiness because I'm now complete,
the doubt I once had I now defeat.
I get lost in your mysterious eyes,
you're so very incredible and that's no lie.
You have the power to make my heart race,
your love is one that I could never replace.
You will always have that affect on me,
and for that I will love you endlessly.
From the first day you had me believing
in love at first sight,
I know it's real
because it feels right.
Nobody else could ever compare,
I'll always cherish the love we share.
I may not have a lot to give you,
only a strong heart brave enough to always stay true.

Storm

I see the lightning and hear the thunder
but see no rain,
maybe this storm will overcome my pain.
Voices roar like thunder filling the empty sky,
holding my ears I close my eyes.
Just like lightning angry faces light up the dark,
hitting the floor, I can no longer feel the beating of my heart.
Tear drops falling endlessly like the sharp rain,
so much hate and so much pain.
Unhealed hearts so afraid to feel,
coming together making nightmares real.
It's too late to ever really understand,
insanely turning down every helping hand.
Because unhappiness and sadness
is what you always bring,
hurting me just don't mean a thing.
You're all acting as if you're so blind,
I made a mistake by falling behind.
It hurts me so much because I never walk away,
I have no answers to why I stay.
I've never felt safe or ever so warm,
especially when it's such a big storm.

Great to Know You

We hit it off great the first day I met you,
you shared what was on your mind and your point of view.
You make it fun to laugh at embarrassing times,
but when it comes to thinking I admire your mind.
You never judge another when they have less,
you never worry and you excuse stress.
You're good to know when days turn bad,
talking with you there's no point to ever be sad.
Because that's just the kind of person you are
to let go of all the things that are negative,
relax and rest
while you continue to think positive.
Everyday it's always so great to know you,
your friendship is one that I'll always hold on to.

I Got You

Capturing the moment you came into sight,
dreaming of you every single night.
Feeling your body move closer to mine,
thinking of your love all the time.
Tasting your lips during your softest kiss,
I've never felt something quite like this.
The feeling of wanting more,
overcomes me like never before.
Tightly wrapping my arms around you I never let go,
tonight the love you have for me you start to show.
I could never imagine it with someone else,
I feel better when I know I got you all to myself.
Falling asleep you hold me tight,
I know that I will never forget this night.

Just Scream

Life is so confusing and tough,
but keep your head up even though times get rough.
Things should get better in a matter of time,
you've made it this far and everything seems to be fine.
Sometimes people pretend that their okay,
and it's always easy to just walk away.
But are they the ones who are insane?
Or are they just not afraid to show other's that they're in pain?
It's hard to feel safe and sometimes content;
but it's real easy to get lost in a certain moment.
The feeling of being alone is always filling that empty space
inside,
if you lose yourself then you'll be left behind.
It's easy to say good-bye but it's hard to let go,
finally hearing the words you already know.
But that's life and how it always seems to be,
so open your eyes and then you will see.
That life can be like a bad dream,
the only way out is to just scream.

I Am Free

I think about the secrets I've not yet told,
now they're getting too unbearable to hold.
I shall let them all go one day,
I shall learn from my mistakes and not run away.
I'll be true to myself and other's around,
I will break through and become the person I need to be.
I hate to think that I am wrong,
but I like to think that I am strong.
I want to change because I don't want to stay the same,
but my honest ways will always remain.
I got to let myself go, heal myself and love
so that it will show.
For I am free I break the chains,
I have let go and there is no more pain.

Starting at the Beginning

You were in my dreams again last night,
we were laughing and smiling and being together felt so right.
That dream made me start to miss you,
starting at the beginning meeting you was too good to be true.
The feeling I got around you was so real,
it was like everything I felt you would feel.
But I'm not the kind who wishes to turn back time,
all I can say is that I was grateful when you were mine.
My imagination got away with me,
on things I wanted to happen and things I wanted to believe.
But if I had to spend the rest of my life
with someone then
it would have to be you,
you were the one who had me believe that love is true,
You had the courage to tell me that you loved me,
I will always believe that we were truly meant to be.

Powerful

Honest and sincere I shall always be,
forever it's going to be you and me.
I can't wait until I start my life with you,
a love we'll create to always be true.
Giving up so much just to gain more,
times with you I'll always adore.
I dream of a life I want to make;
all the chances I will take.
In order to have you beside me,
I dream of you only.
I believe that this is something we both need,
this is something in which we can succeed.
It doesn't matter if it's right or wrong,
loving you gives me strength to be strong.
The only person I see is you,
my love will always be so powerful and true.

Stop

Spin around until I drop,
faster and faster I reach the top.
Around I go my feet meets the floor,
I can't stop now I want to gain more.
Dizziness over comes me before I close my eyes,
laughter gets strong there are no more cries.
Step after step I start to dance,
I never thought I would take that chance.
Changing along with each year,
now knowing you don't have to be here.
I'm stronger with you,
I changed my life I made it through.
It gets better after all,
no matter how hard it gets I will not fall.
Spin around I've reached the top,
faster and faster I will not stop.

One More Reason

I listen to the whispers of the night,
I feel the warmth of your arms when you hold me tight.
Feeling the softness of your lips with the most beautiful kiss,
telling me I'm your most deepest wish.
No other in this world could ever compare,
the love I want is the love we share.
Making you my biggest desire grows stronger each day,
your tender touch takes me way.
Amazingly falling deeper in love with you
is more than I'll ever need,
never stressing because you'll always have me.
I'll try harder each day to never lose you,
turns out after all that your heart is true.
Distracting me and I can't clear my mind,
so much comfort in you is what I always find.
You've helped me to be less doubtful,
you touch and cherish my soul.
One out of a million turns out to be true,
one more reason to why I love you.

Something

I keep on going with each day,
through it all I'll be Okay.
Because I know that you'll soon be mine,
I just need to give it time.
If I force it then there's a chance
that it could never be,
and I really want you to be with me.
So I'm going to be patient and just wait,
because once I have you our love will be great.
Greater then all the love in the world
with just a single touch,
I'll fall every day and you'll grow to love me so much.
It will happen because that's what I feel,
I'll pursue this dream and make you real.
You'll come for me and rescue my heart,
we'll feel the same until the end like we will in the start.
You'll have me and I'll have you,
every day we'll have something to hold on to.

A Little Space

I'm just another person in this world,
some call me a woman but I feel like a little girl.
What makes me so different from everyone else?
I'm my own person I'm just myself.
I like to follow my own rules and go my own way,
the way I am is the way I'm going to stay.
I use to live with my eyes closed but now they' re open,
I keep my heart to myself because it has been broken.
But that doesn't mean it's the end of the world
because life goes on,
and I'm trying to figure out
where I really belong.
I know that in a matter of time
I'm sure to find my place,
but for now all I need
is just a little space.

I Want to Know

You're so very beautiful in every possible way,
I know I'll be with you one day.
Because I can feel it in my heart,
I fell for you in the start.
I needed you for so long,
I want to take this chance before it's gone.
I now know what I must do,
and that is tell all my feelings to you.
Talking with you and hours go by,
no one else just you and I.
I need to find out if you feel the same,
because I'm not the type to play games.
There's just so much I want to know,
like why I can't ever let you go?

Sweet Romance

I sent to you my love letter,

saying that I'll love you forever.

I gave to you all my heart,

but I realize that we're apart.

I say to you that I'll love you more,

never once have I fell before,

But all I need from you,

is a love remarkable and so very true.

I kiss your lips and I begin to fall,

if I can't have you then I want nothing at all.

I feel your body close to me,

I want to be the only one you see.

I breathe you in just to live,

I return to you all that you give.

I fear not to love you so give me one chance,

I'll fill your world with sweet romance.

I crave your touch all the time,

I need for you to be just mine.

Prepared

Finally I have learned to let go,
the new me begins to grow.
Each day I will stand tall,
and smile like I have it all
Even though I don't but it's nice to dream,
because all I really do have is just me.
I'm happy in my own way,
life goes on with everyday.
So I know that I'm going to be okay
I'll make it through,
well only if I continue to look up to you.
Teach me how to be strong,
and stop me before I am wrong.
I'm beginning to understand more,
on what I want for sure.
I can't stand no more mistakes,
I don't care what it takes.
Because this time I am prepared,
now I know that I can't be scared.

Create a Life

Remembering all the chances I never took,
makes me turn back for just one last look.
All the things I needed to say I should have said,
now I can't get my past out of my head.
Memories come back and it's so hard to forget,
mistakes appear and I begin to regret.
I got to get away from it all,
I do not answer when the nightmares call.
It hurts to know that they' re all acting
as if they don't know me,
I wonder if this is how it's supposed to be.
I'll take my life and make the best of it every day,
and everything I feel I will say.
A new beginning is sure to start,
I'll create a life I see in my heart.

I Finally Have You

Spending a lifetime with you is my dream,
my wish is for you to love me.
I got to think positive when it comes to me and you,
because one day my dream is bound to come true.
Our love will live forever because it will be strong,
we'll love each other more and always hold on.
My chants and prayers are sent out,
we'll live for each other and love without doubt.
I know we can do this we just have to try,
we shouldn't let this chance pass us by.
I can feel my dream coming true,
I'll be so happy when I finally have you.
Let's take this chance just to see,
if we are meant to be.

My Place

I won't let you down when it comes to loving you,
I'll make sure you know my love is true.
I can't imagine how life would be
without you beside me,
I want this life that I need.
I was so amazed by your gentle touch,
I still haven't found out how I love you so much.
But in time I will know,
because even after a lifetime
I still won't let you go.
I know in my heart that you're the one for me,
wherever you are is where I'll be.
You'll never be alone because I'll always be there,
everything of mine I'll forever share.
Even my life because I'm living for two now,
and to get through you showed me how.
I have found my place,
it's where I can always see your face
and feel your embrace.

You Caught Me

I love you more after every touch,

having your heart made me change so much.

I've changed for the better,

just so you and I could be together.

Dreaming magic between me and you,

there's nothing else that could be this true.

I close my eyes and your face I can see,

I treasure the love between you and me.

These will be known as my happiest days,

touching you in so many ways,

My life with you I will forever share,

you'll never be alone because I'll always be there.

Our bodies and souls will never part,

with open arms I give you my heart.

You caught me before I fell down,

I'm never alone because you're always around.

Long Gone

If only you'd listen then you would understand,
if you don't have the time then don't lend a hand.
Don't say you'll be there if you won't,
don't say you'll do something and then don't.
Because that can tear someone apart,
it hurts to be the one with the broken heart.
Don't make promises that will turn into lies,
don't say you'll love me forever
because what if the love dies?
I don't ever want to hate you so don't make me,
I've tried so hard but I can't believe.
You have to stand up tall and be strong,
don't give up go on.
Some things just happen for the better,
so don't stress it because it won't last forever.
Forget about everything that has ever went wrong,
focus on the future because the past is long gone.
Clear your mind and remember me,
don't forget that you* re the one I need.

But

I could never tell you a lie,
I could never walk away when you need to cry.
I would never laugh at you if you got hurt in anyway,
I would never have the heart to try to make you stay.
I will never try to make you love me,
I will never say we are meant to be.
I have never hated you,
I have never told you anything that wasn't true.
But...
I could tell you that I love you with all my heart,
I could promise you that we'll never be apart.
I would always let you know how much you mean to me,
I would live just to know you're all I need.
I will always tell you the truth
about anything you want to know,
I will always hold on and never let go.
I have the courage to be able to share a life with you,
I have a dream that I want to make come true.

Used to Be

I'm out of sight and out of mind,

the memories of me you left behind.

Just because I'm not there doesn't mean I'm gone,

I guess I'm the one still holding on.

That's only because I miss you so much

and I can't let go,

the way I feel you will never know.

Because you keep on pushing me away,

it hurts me too because I couldn't stay.

If I had a choice

you know that I would still be there,

but it seems as if you don't care.

So maybe we did grow apart,

but that doesn't mean you're not in my heart.

Because you are and always will be,

I hate to think that you've forgotten about me.

I really hope you haven't

because I remember you,

I remember all the things that we've been through.

I just wish you would talk to me,

because it's okay to look back on how we used to be.

Always Loved

Often wondering if you're my soul mate,
we'll be brought together because it's our fate.
I wait for you all day long,
I know you're out there I must hold on.
Knowing that we will be together,
reuniting our souls forever.
Needing to feel you next to me,
forever I know that we will be.
Dreaming of the day when I see your face,
no other could take your place.
I'll be your honest lover until the end of time,
this dream I take and make mine.
I know you're waiting for me and it won't be much longer,
between the distance we can feel it's getting stronger.
Because in our hearts we know the meaning of it all,
today and for the rest of my life love calls.
Answering to it so faithfully and proud,
opening our eyes we are finally found.
We're the one's who know it's true,
because from the very first day I have always loved you.

Each Other

Loving one another we could never go wrong,
this is where we belong.
Holding you I hold everything,
another year goes by seeing what the future will bring.
Never wanting this to end,
you're not only my soul mate you're my best friend.
Feeling so safe with you, you're my dream that came true.
Tenderness is always in your every touch,
I don't know what it is but I love you so much.
It should never matter the color,
the only thing that does is that we love each other.

Future with You

I encourage in all you do,
I find myself deeply in love with you.
Wanting to have us to be all alone,
by ourselves emotions are shown.
Come a little bit closer for me to see,
the one I love endlessly.
I really want to get to know you and spend more time,
I want to get personal but not cross the line.
Because I want you to feel comfortable around me,
but when I look at you I see a mystery.
I want to be the other half of you,
for never a day I'll be untrue.
I need to feel excitement and I want it all,
because you're the one who caused me to fall.
Have no worry for I do not lie,
feel no more pain and never again cry.
Because I thought it all through,
and I want a future with you.

Breathe

I hear your voice turn into music
and I can't breathe,
so beautiful I find it hard to believe.
I want to be in your heart,
forever having our mind and soul
to never be apart.
I never felt something so strong,
if I'm happy then it can't be wrong.
I know that many people don't really understand,
but I'm so proud to hold your hand,
That's something I can only share with you,
it's just not the same with anyone else
because with you it's true.
Every time I see your face
my secret love song plays in my mind,
I can't believe that you were so hard to find.
I want it to be only you and me,
I close my eyes and I breathe.
I never want to let you go,
that's just something I had to let you know.

Moments with You

I love you so much words can't describe,
needing you I can't lie.
Seeing your face I wish you were here,
being with you I have no fear.
Just imagine the way I feel,
knowing the truth it's all real.
All these emotions comes from so deep within,
take me to a place I have never been.
Feeling so happy I have no reasons to cry,
falling for you I can't deny.
I want to feel you close to me,
I have to know that you'll never leave.
Fall asleep in my arms forever more,
the moments with you I will always adore.

My Song

No to love is what I may say,

but I could never turn you away.

And the reason why I'll never know,

the feeling you give me is too strong to let go.

I want to say that I've never felt this way before,

so what could go wrong if I said it once more?

For all that you are I do care,

I never want to miss you I want to always be there.

I want this feeling to always stay the same,

I want us to always and forever remain.

Letting it all out from keeping it all inside,

always to be found and never have to hide.

From my dark fear I do walk out,

loving you I have no doubt.

You're my song I play in my heart,

I run into the light and run from the dark

I love you so very much,

I could never have a want to feel another's touch.

How It Should Be

Let me tell you a little about me,
let me show you what I see.
All day long I sit and stare,
at others who are so unfair.
I don't understand how others can be so mean,
there is so much hate and judgment that I've seen.
I ask of you to be kind,
but yet lies I still find.
I need to know what I can do,
to make it easier for others to get through.
Every second of each day I lend my hand,
catch their fall and listen to understand.
I can hear you loud and clear,
I bring to you strength to defeat your fears.
Being good to others is how it should be,
there's so much beauty open your eyes to see.

The Lost Courage

Hear me when I cry at night,
be Mother's arms that hold me tight.
Bring me up when I fall down,
come to me when no one else is around.
Take me by the hand,
and say that you will always understand.
Listen to the words that I speak,
give me courage when I'm scared and weak.
Let me know that you are here,
help me get rid of my biggest fear.
Promising me that I'll never be harmed,
running to Mother when she's open arms.
Loving you with every second
when my heart beats inside my chest,
knowing that it's time for
 leave me me to let go and rest.
Please don't ever behind,
help me achieve and get the lost courage I must find.

What You Feel

I want to be your everything every day,
hold on to me so the feelings won't go away.
Feel it in your heart how much I mean to you,
tell me that you love me too.
Then swear it until the end of time,
let me make you mine.
I want to feel that you'll never let me go,
tell me your feelings so that I know.
Promise me that you'll never break my heart,
need me until the end like you did in the start.
All I want is a true love only from you,
tell me that it can be true.
If you can give that to me,
then I can say we are meant to be.
Make your heart be real,
give to me what you feel.

Every Night

I find myself regretting the small things
that I should've said before,
all the memories get lost
and I start to fall more.
So I begin to write down all I know,
so far it's been easy being alone.
I've thought about how it would be
if I was with someone else,
but I've made it this far depending on myself.
I guess this is how I will always be,
walking alone and just being me.
I've got so much more to do,
even if it means doing it without you.
I know that I will be okay,
because after every night there is a new day.
I'll go to sleep tonight,
knowing that tomorrow will be all right.

Now

Singing just to remember her,
picturing your face but all I see is a blur.
This can't be happening how can this be?
I need you to remember me.
Don't let my memory die,
stop me before I cry.
Because crying keeps me up all night,
none of this feels right.
I close my eyes to go blind,
I sit here and clear my mind.
I need not worry but I don't know how,
does my life begin now?
Or do I have to sit here and wait?
And regret how I was too late?
Too late to catch your fall,
acting deaf so I couldn't hear you call.
I'm sorry that I did this to you,
now there's nothing I can do.

Define

You gave me so many reasons to hold on,
you gave me strength to stay strong.
You're my heart that beats every day,
breathing you, takes my breath away.
You listen to how I feel,
the love I wanted you made it real.
I know I'm not blind because I can see you,
you' re so real you became true.
You've given me a life so meaningful,
you love my heart and my soul.
I was finally found by another honest heart,
one who has loved me from the start.
There's nobody else just you and me,
different truths for us to see.
I love you more with every second, minute, and hour,
you give my heart so much power.
Define the way I feel for you,
take the love I give is true.

Fly

Falling forever as I take flight,
breaking through the clouds comes in the sunlight.
Another beautiful morning and I start to plan my day,
all my worries and fears get lifted away.
With the wind in my face I close my eyes,
I hold out my arms and I begin to fly.
Looking so far down I can see you below,
time goes by so fast but it seems so slow.
Getting closer to reaching freedom it's been so long,
disappearing in the sky I'll forever be gone.
Waking up and I rub my eyes,
I guess my biggest dream is to be able to fly.

A Love

Mother you're my light in the dark,
forever I give to you my heart.
Past the years you gave so much to me,
there's no other love that is this complete.
I've learned so much from you,
you helped me out when I needed to get through.
I'll love you until my dying day,
because even after death this love will stay.
Everything I know you taught to me,
your love is all I'll ever need.
With you besides me I feel like I have it all,
you have always encouraged me to stand tall.
No matter how old I get I'll always need you,
that's one thing I always knew.
The greatest kind of love that you could ever feel
is a Mother's,
a love compared to that
there is no other.

Might As well

I got to run to get away,
in order to leave I can't stay.
I'm sure that you understand me,
this is how I will always be.
I've realized that I'm so far behind,
but never once do I seem to mind.
All I know is that I have to be strong,
I know my rights from all my wrong•
There's a lot of chances I didn't take,
but I have always learned from my mistakes.
No matter how old I get
I'll always learn something new,
I know so many people who are false
and so very little who are true.
I'm not ashamed to admit
that there is still so much that I don't know,
but that's never a good reason
to give up or let go.
It's just how I look at life as I move on,
and through it all I've gotten strong.
I think I might as well just stay,
because I don't want to run I'd rather walk away.

I'm Not Blind

If only you could take my place
and see through my eyes,
it's hard to act deaf
when you hear all their cries.
You can't find comfort no matter where you look
how much can you take,
until you give in and break?
I begin to lose hope with the more I see,
I then ask myself why do I have to be me?
I had the choice to either leave or stay,
I still question myself to why I never walked away.
What can you do when no one seems to care?
All of this is nowhere near fair.
The people who needed help were left alone,
and emotionally they can't fix it on their own.
I now know I'm not blind,
all this has really opened my mind.
I thought my mind was open before,
this just seems to have opened it more.

From My Heart

I'm not perfect and that you can see,
no one is perfect so it's not just me.
1 know I've made mistakes before,
and I realize that down the road I'll make more.
I have had doubts and worries on my mind,
that's why I leave my past behind.
I may not have gotten that far on my own,
but I do know that I can make it alone.
I have finally learned to move on,
I build myself to be strong.
Now I look at life from a different point of view,
I'll make some changes even if it's just a few.
I take some courage to make a dream come true,
expressions from my heart I wish to share with all of you.
My voice shall be heard loud and clear,
hear my promises that are loyal and sincere.

Another Day

Waking up to a new day,
wondering what's going to come my way.
I love to wonder but I hate to wait;
another success and it feels so great.
I can't believe I got this far just to gain more,
the feeling of beauty I haven't felt before.
So far ahead and I chose not to look behind,
everything in my past don't ever cross my mind.
To the top I finally broke through,
you were never there so I forgot about you.
I can feel it as if it's already real,
it's not a joke because it's how I feel.
I need this more than anything right now,
and to be able to love I know how.
I am everything put into one,
there's no going back because once it's over it's done.
And I know that I'll make it through another day,
because I can see what's coming my way.

When I Found

I want to spend the rest of my life loving you,
to be honest there's nothing else I'd rather do.
I will confess that I dream of you every night,
even when you're beside me holding me tight.
Because you make my dreams so much sweeter
when you are here,
and to be declined never will
that you have to fear.
That's because I love you for the person that you are,
I never love you less when you are far.
So I give to you my soul and heart,
they've been yours from the start.
Feeling your love is the greatest
that I could ever feel,
it changed my life
when I found out that you are for real.

Made It Real

Surviving off the goodness of your heart,
trying to explain my love where do I start?
I will not question the way I feel for you,
because I have a feeling that it's true.
I dream of a life involving you and me,
I wonder if it will ever be.
I can hear you whispering from a distance away,
I hear your every thought that you say.
Making love to you is like a dream,
my wish came true because you're here with me.
Our love will never end,
because in you I have found it all
even a best friend.
It's the best feeling I could ever feel,
honest love and you made it real.
You proved me wrong when you stole my heart,
I've always belonged to you from the start.

When the Time Comes

Heartbeats are racing and blood flowing,

confused minds but our hearts still knowing.

Emotions and slow movements growing to be strong,

I try to let go but I'm still holding on.

I'm addicted to you and it feels real good,

if I can be what you want I would if I could.

My desire is strong and very intense,

making love to you but not loving you wouldn't make any sense.

Because I do love you, this I can prove.

There is only one person in this world that I'll ever need,

that is you loving me.

Such an amazing love I can't deny,

trust in me because the heart doesn't lie.

When the time comes it will show,

through it all we never let go.

Good Friends

My love for you still goes on,
your strength continues to keep me strong.
The impact you put in my life I will never forget,
good memories are hard to regret.
I miss you like crazy and I will more each day,
the thoughts of you don't go away.
Hopefully I'll see you again I hope it will be soon,
I think of you with each new moon.
You got me wishing to turn back time,
I'm glad that you're a friend of mine.
I'll remember you until the end,
in my heart we will always be good friends.
I know that things won't ever be the same,
but at least the heartwarming memories will always remain.

The Last

For you my love I give it all,
I'll be behind you to always catch your fall.
Trust in me because I won't let you down,
I'm so happy that it was you I found.
I promise to be faithful as long as I live,
only affection I will give.
I just want to be with you,
I've never felt love this true.
I need you in my life like I need air to breathe,
because loving you is all I need.
You've touched my heart and have made it last,
building our future to remember our past.
This is the happiest that I've ever been,
this love began when I let you in.

Three Words

Words to explain "I love you," this won't be easy to do.
There are millions of words that I could say,
but would they help me steal your heart away?
so many questions
that need to be answered by only one,
what comes next after that's done?
Could I win if I tell you
I think of you every day and night?
What about saying it's a dream
to hold you tight?
What about telling you every second how I feel?
Every hour I'll prove that I'm for real.
I know, how about saying you're the only one I live for?
I want to be with you forever more.
There are millions of words I want to say,
so have I yet stole your heart away?
See, I told you that explaining all this
would not be easy to do,
so I think I'll just stick with the three words
"I love you."

Have It All

Taking time to love you right,
needing you here to hold me tight.
Dreaming of you I take you by the hand,
your every word I listen that's how I understand.
You walked into my life and I'll always remember you,
I have so much interest in what you do.
Breathing you I start to feel you close to me,
there's nowhere else I'd rather be.
Because I got you right here in my heart,
I've longed for you from the start.
Now I got you and won't let you go,
I just can't ever tell you no.
Caressing your body so tender and so very much,
I love to wake up to your soft touch.
But I can't help it because I'm all for you,
so much to give and ever so true.
Falling backwards and you catch my fall,
with you emotionally I have it all.

Time of Day

Love yourself and others around you,
be good to others and be true.
You'll be surprised
how good you'll feel about yourself,
and it's because you're honest to someone else.
Love is a good feeling
when it's returned in the right way,
true words are beautiful
when they're said in the sincere way.
Needing to be held then just open your arms,
bring to no one harm.
Open your heart and free your mind,
the truth is what you will find.
That you are just like me,
the real you is who you need to be.
Judging should never be done in anyway,
give others a chance and give them the time of day.

Much Pride

Your company is the greatest that I've ever known,
you're always around when I feel alone.
You're a great friend and always will be,
you seemed to have learned how to understand me.
I smile to the fact of knowing
all the times spent with you,
you made hard times easy to get through.
I love to listen to your mind and heart,
you have been an incredible person from the start.
To find a friend I don't have to look far,
because when I open my eyes there you are.
In you I have found it all,
so much to say with just one call.
It's great to have you by my side,
I stand beside you with so much pride.

Yet to Start

You're my reason to wake up every day,
you're the reason to why I can't ever walk away.
It's amazing on how much I truly love you,
it's incredible how you're always true.
For all that you are I will always hold on,
and with all my strength I will stay strong.
Every day you'll see I'll always try,
I'll never have a good enough reason to ever lie.
Because the truth is what you will always hear,
I'll always hold you near.
Our every moment I love to share,
no matter what happens I will always care.
Because I love you with all my heart,
my life is yet to start.
With you beside me,
you're where I will always be.

Our Love

Thinking of you makes my day seem better,
believing your promise when you said forever.
I know I love you for real,
with you there's so much to feel.
I get lost every time
you hold me in your embrace,
I never saw such beauty until I saw your face.
I never felt so safe until you held my hand,
I feel so understood because you understand.
You let me know that you care}
I never have to worry because you're always there.
Your love means so much to me,
you're the only person I'll ever need.
The only one I see is you,
you're my dream that has finally come true.
I can't live without you
so I won't even try,
my life got better
with just one look in your eyes.
I know that our love will never end,
because we're not only lovers but also best friends.

Passionately Strong

Finding the right words to describe
the best way I feel about you,
will be words of my heart
that will always be true.
I want to be able to bring happiness
into your life forever more,
I think I've found
what I've been looking for.
Seeing no distance when I look in your eyes,
gives me the strength to always try.
Needing to hold you so close to me,
I really want to believe that we are meant to be.
Because this feeling gets stronger
every time I'm around you,
forever I want it to be just us two.
Hearing the truth of your brave heart;
you were strong enough to love me from the start.
Take me to your world and touch my soul so deep,
these are the moments in my life I'll always keep.
Have me be your biggest wish
and sweetest dream come true,

let me forever love you.
Because I sing about our love
that is passionately strong,
our life together
is my deepest love song.

Just Seconds

Falling apart as time flies by,
the truth hurts but it's hard to lie.
You allowed my heart to fall for you,
now what am I supposed to do?
I hate to know
that I'm falling in love with you more each day,
I only pray for you to not walk away.
The power of your touch has taken over me,
the truth in your words I die to need.
I find warmth inside of you,
you give me something to hold on to.
You have a beautiful heart as well as mind,
I have no reason to fall behind.
Because you stand right beside me through it all,
you're always here in just seconds when I call.

I Fell

I hear you calling from far away,
I turn around and I choose to stay.
I never thought that this could happen to me,
to find someone I really need.
I never dreamed that love could feel this way
until I saw you,
I never thought I'd find someone so true.
I close my eyes and I feel your embrace,
I look up and see your beautiful face.
Just one look in your eyes caused me to fall,
forever more I give you my all.
You were in my heart in a short amount of time,
now I'm yours and you are mine.
I'm so happy I don't know who to tell,
I'm so glad that I fell.

In My Life

You stole my heart when you looked in my eyes,
you caught my fall and heard my cries.
I never thought
that I could love someone so much,
you made me fall with your tender touch.
You make my heart sing many tunes,
I've never thought that this could be true.
Because I love you too much to be able to explain,
there is nothing about you that I would change.
Seeing you smile just brightens my day,
I never want these feelings to go away.
I have all these desires going through my mind,
ones that I never thought I would find.
For you're in my life and I'll never let go,
I need you so much I love you so.

The Way You Do

You picked me up just on time,
this is the night you became mine.
So romantic I couldn't believe my eyes,
I'm falling for you and that I can't lie.
You had this whole night planned out
for just me and you,
all I ever wanted just came true.
A night with just us all alone,
wanting it to last forever
I don't want to go home.
Finally realizing that this is where I truly belong,
holding you close these feelings become strong.
You're the one I've been waiting for,
with all that you are I could never want more.
Because I got it all by just having you,
thanks for loving me the way you do.

Will Never Be

Run away with me,

forget how life is supposed to be,

Take me I'm yours,

every day you'll love me more.

Take my heart it belongs to you,

feel the way I do.

Hear my whispers every night,

know that this is all right.

Breathe the tune that my heart plays,

feel the truth with me you'll stay.

I love you too much but let me explain,

true love is worth to gain.

Close your eyes and let it be known,

that our hearts will never be alone.

Single Breath

You keep me wishing to be next to you,
you have me wanting all this to be true.
I got to get away to you somehow I'll find a way,
because there's just so much I need to say.
You're my dreams that I've made,
all these desires will never fade.
I create the sweetest dream of you and me,
taking the excitement we'll always be.
Holding your heart next to my chest,
the love you give is the best.
But that's all a dream that I'll someday make true,
it won't be too long now until I have you.
We'll be together and never part,
your single breath takes my heart.

Feed

I feel you breathing right next to me,

I close my eyes and it's your face that I see.

I want to be the right one for you,

I want to be there for whatever you may go through.

I love each day that passes by,

I'm with you with no good-byes.

My life has become a dream come true,

it all began when I found you.

I need the way you make me feel,

in your arms my heart you heal.

Only you I am here for,

to only you I give more.

Because you know how I feel inside,

you make me not want to hide.

You my love I will always need,

for my hungry heart you always feed.

My Promise

With my eyes I watch your every move,
with my lips I softly whisper I love you.
With my arms I'll hold you tight,
just to comfort you I'll stay all night.
And with my body I lay it next to yours,
if it had not been for you I'd have nothing to live for.
Tall and proud I will stand,
I wake up every day just to hold your hand.
As long as I get to see your face,
this world will continue to be such a wonderful place.
I want my every moment to be spend with you,
there is so much more I want to say and do.
With just one look you stole my heart away,
with you is where I'll always stay.
This is my promise that will forever stay true,
now you promise that I will always have you.

Have Me

When the dark rolls in to take the light;
I'll be by your side all night.
I'll hold you close without letting go,
the gentlest touch I will show.
Be close at heart all the time,
be sure to tell me that you are mine.
I love you and need you forever more,
all this is way more different from before.
Very first day I knew my heart would heal,
the love you give me is more than real.
I can't sit back and watch you walk away,
give me time to find the right words to say.
You know that you have mej
I'm right where I want to be.

Break Through

Call me crazy but I would die for you,
lay down my heart and forever be true.
Offering my life just to save yours,
I'll never give less I'll always give more.
Loving you I could never be wrong,
be honest and true show me you're strong.
Deeply caress my heart and soulj
give me love that is so meaningful,
Without you I'm afraid I'll go insane,
believe that I could never cause you pain.
I'm not here to be hurtful or unreal,
because there has been so much love for me to feel.
With you is where I'll always be,
I want to be the one you will always need.
Help me to break through,
be nobody else but you.

Emotions I Can't Feel

Falling asleep to the sound of your voice,
has me believing that I made the right choice.
Every sun rise I seem to love you more,
your every breath is what I live for.
Being with you there's no emotions I can't feel,
I can't believe this is real.
Because everyday feels like a dream come true,
where would I be if I didn't have you?
You've showed me that you' re one of a kind,
and for that I'll never leave you behind.
Because I need you and the love you give,
I found my reason to live.

Staying

It's been so long since I've felt your touch,
there is just something about you
that makes me love you so much.
I long to hear your voice and see your face,
you're a part of me
that I could never replace.
It's like I've almost forgotten the taste of you,
that's one thing I look forward to.
There's so many things I'd like you to know,
and above all I'll never let you go.
There will never be a single day,
when any of these feelings go away.
Every second a little bit of my love I will share,
every minute I'll show you how much I care.
There is nothing from you that I will ever hide,
because the only thing that matters is that I'm by your side.
The only thing that can help me prove
how much I love you,
is staying faithful and true.

Think Twice

I love to dream of you every night,
you make all these emotions feel so right.
I now know what I want and it's you,
there's nothing that I won't go through.
I wish to touch you but you're too far,
I know you can feel it in your heart
that I love you for who you are.
I could never leave or let you go,
because there's so much of me that I want to show.
It's so pleasant to hear you laugh and see you smile,
you are sure worth the while.
I need you to be next to me,
you're the only one I need to see.
Being with you I don't need to think twice,
having you really feels nice.

I Remember

I remember every little thing you would do,
I remember you.
I remember all the things you would say;
I remember staying with you that one day.
I remember the very first day I met you
and how you had me felt,
just being around you made my heart melt.
I remember every small face impression you made,
and how slowly they would fade.
I remember the sound of your voice,
I remember how you became my very first choice.
I remember how I used to wish
that I could be with you,
1 really hope that you've remembered me too.

A Special Place

Once again I got left behind,

emotions and feelings cloud my mind.

I get lost in the moment and never seem to realize,

that you never once looked in my eyes.

Because if you would then you'd already see,

that the one standing here is me.

You pushed me to keep my head up and to be strong,

after everything I'm still holding on.

You got the best out of me and you barely had to try,

I guess my intuition didn't lie.

Now I got something to look forward to everyday,

you're my inspiration that will never go away.

A special place for me is in your heart,

you noticed me in the start.

Best Friend

In you is where you'll find my heart,
from you I will never part.
Because I can't seem to breathe without you,
you stole my dream and made it true.
Gently you hold me in your embrace,
one more memory to never erase.
Our hearts beating softly together
puts me in a deep sleep,
all your love I put in my heart to always keep.
Dedicating myself to only you,
never have to worry because I'll always be true.
Sincerely I give my love to you always,
you took away all my lonely days.
To you I will always return all the love
that you give to me,
honest and faithful I'll forever be.
I want to make you happy until the end,
because you're my companion for life
and my best friend.

Let Go of You

A certain person changed my life for the better,
I remember that there was never a day
when we weren't together.
I can't forget the song that played in my heart
every time I saw you,
there was never a day when you were untrue.
That's why I'm writing this poem for you
just to say,
I love and miss you every day.
I wish that I could take back
all the wrong and make it right,
I wish you were close enough to be in sight.
I miss the feeling I would get every time
I looked into your eyes,
I hurt you and that I didn't realize.
I never meant to hurt you and now it's hard to live,
just to see you again
there's nothing I wouldn't give.
I lost that certain person
who changed my life for the better,
but he'll always be in my heart forever.
I know what I must do,
and that is I have to let go of you.

You

You want to leave but yet you stay,
you want to hide and run away.
You tell me secrets that you know I'll keep,
you come to me when you're in too deep.
You ask me questions that I don't know,
you even express emotions you feel you need to show.
You know that I will always be here for you,
you know my friendship will always be true.
When you settled for less I have always gave more,
you know that you got my heart for sure.
You feel that you can trust me so you let me in,
and with it all you fight just to win.
You got to know that it's okay to be wrong,
you're human and life goes on.

Feel It

Showing me you love me more,
gets more intense than before.
Loving the feeling you always give,
gives me more of a reason to live.
Wanting and needing you so very much,
takes over me every time we touch.
Slowly moving closer to you,
tells you that my love is true.
Embracing your every movement I hold you tight,
feeling it's real because it feels right.
Intentions grow stronger between us
with each passing day,
I don't think it's possible
for this feeling to ever go away.
Emotionally I know that I have you,
because I can really feel it too.
You're the one for me I know,
because I can't ever let you go.

Give Me a Chance

Call on me when you need to smile,
let me walk that extra mile.
Have me want you more each day,
tell me the things I'd only wish you would say.
Convince me that what you say is true,
let me be able to love only you.
Cry to me when you' re feeling sad,
give me a chance to keep something I have never had.
Let me take care of you
and have you take whatever I may give,
and give me a life I can finally love to live.
I'll heal your heart whenever it aches,
even if it takes my own heart to break.
I'll be your strength when you're feeling weak,
and the words you long to hear I will always speak.
You're my cure when I go insane,
you're my drug to stop my pain.
Make me feel as if this is all brand new,
as long as I'm only with you.

Without You

Gentle loving is what you give to me,

you're the kind who knows what I need.

Loving you to no end, it's hard to believe

that we used to be just friends.

When I need someone to talk to you are there,

you have your own way to show me that you care.

I think of you day in and day out,

you're the only one I dream about.

Other's might not see what I do,

that's why they'll never understand how much I love you.

I know my feelings for you will always remain,

I just hope that for you it's the same.

Because I do love you with all my heart,

I need to be close to you and not too far apart.

I know my life would never be the same without you,

can this all really be true?

What We Could

Dreaming of you makes me feel better,
wishing for you knowing we'll be together.
I have so much to give to you,
give me a chance to show you I'm true.
There's so many emotions I want to make you feel,
I'll give you something that is real.
Tell me that I can have you,
let me show you what I can do.
Wanting to have me then I'm all yours,
nobody else could love you more.
Because I am all about you every day,
that's something no one can take away.
I want you here with me,
I'll give you love that you can believe.
This is a chance we should take,
there's no telling what we could make.

Your World

You're my one true love in my heart,
always together and never apart.
Loving you more and more each day,
because I know these feelings won't go away.
I will always stand tall and proud,
to all the strong love that I have found.
Everything that I've always wanted in love
I have found in you,
with you beside me there's nothing I can't do.
You've given me hope when I thought it was gone,
no matter what to you I will always hold on.
Because I never want to lose you in a lifetime,
you've made me a part of your world so here is mine.
I give it to you with great love and all my trust,
the endless happiness you shared with me
has filled my heart up.
I always wanted to be your one and only girl,
because the most wonderful place I want to be
is in your world.

If You

If you would ask me how much I love you
I'd say with all my heart,
I'd explain how I felt from the start:
If you would ask me how long I've loved you
I'd say forever,
if you want to we can stay together.
If you would want to hold and comfort me
I would say it would be all right,
if you would ask me I'd stay all night.
If you want to get closer to me,
then if that's what you want I'd let it be.
If you want it all then just say so,
if you'd like I won't ever let you go,
If you want I could love you,
just the way you would want me to.

Being You

If a man is strong enough to love me,
then that is all I will ever need.
I don't want big houses money or cars,
all I want is you for who you are.
I don't need or want all those things,
and I could care less about any diamond rings.
All I want is someone to love me for me,
someone who could convince me to believe.
Believe in trust and happiness and all of the above,
the one and only true love.
I would never treat you wrong,
I would never let go I would hold on.
Because if you don't have a big house
money, or a car,
that still wouldn't make me go far.
So please see me as I am,
because I'll tell you I love you
once I see you again.
You have nothing to prove,
because you won my heart by just being you.

Someone to Love

All of this time I had you,
and after so long I still can't believe it's true.
You make me feel new in so many ways,
the intentions between you and me stays.
Knowing that there's no time
to think about what's right and wrong,
never could care
because it's been so long.
Memories rush through this mind of mine,
realizing that it's now our time.
Counting the hours that pass us by,
life is better when it's just you and I,
Being in your arms every chance I get,
now seeing that you're someone to love
without regret.

Isn't Too Late

Remembering good times that involved you,
I often wonder what you' re up to.
It's been three years but it feels like forever,
you always knew how to make things better.
But I keep you in my heart to no end,
in you I've always found an honest friend.
I will remember you
and continue to miss you more every day,
the times I needed you
never once did you walk away.
I know that in the future
I'll meet up with you,
because forgetting you I just can't do.
It would be so nice to get to see you again,
and to that I always seem to ask myself when?
There's no such thing in time to wait,
because even forever isn't too late.

In the Stars

Taking the chance so I could be with you,
no matter what we'll always get through,
Wanting us to live happy and strong,
keeps me forever holding on.
Looking in your eyes I can see it all,
rough times won't ever make us fall.
Because we'll always have each other and that's
for sure, no one else I could ever love more.
I can't deny this because I know it's all true,
written in the stars I am meant for you.
We've gotten this far and we continue to move on,
I will not doubt it because this feeling has stayed long.
All we need to do
is build onto the Jove more every day,
because then there will be no chance
for the love to be taken away.
And that is what I will always believe,
I've felt from the start that you were meant for me.

I Ask Why

Can you see me like I can see you?

Do you hear me trying to get through?

I've had the chance to let you know,

but I got scared and I let you go.

How can I go about to fix this mistake?

How do you heal a heart that always seems to break?

It seems to be difficult all the way,

and I've forgotten all the words I wanted to say.

The more I see you the harder it gets to realize,

that the pain I caused made you cry.

I'm the one who let go

and I'm the one who is left to pay,

if I could have just one wish

I would have never walked away.

Why does falling in love build and create fear?

I should have let you in and kept you near.

So I guess this time I'll say good-bye,

I'm not going to wonder nor will I ask why.

I'm in Touch

To control my emotions takes self-defense,
to get confused makes no sense.
Back away from me so I can breathe,
get out of my face I want to see.
Depression causes serious pressure on my brain,
silence seems to keep me sane.
What I don't get is not knowing how to break free,
you abuse the word love and then spread it like a disease.
You look at me like I'm a failure
with all the small choices I make,
even my right moves you label as mistakes.
If you don't have nothing but hate to share
then just turn around,
because years ago I've left that damn playground.
But you never will because you've stayed the same,
your face is fading
and I don't recall remembering your name.
Don't treat me like I'm stupid
because I'm far from that,
if you want it in writing
then I'll lay down the facts.
I got the right state of mind to be in control,
I know myself and I'm in touch with my soul.

Magic

Spirits of nature made by our Mother earth,

if only us humans could see what you're truly worth.

Beautiful fairies stir up the air,

embracing your energy I feel that you're there.

The element of fire come light the darkest night,

lift my soul to the higher heights.

Thirst comes from water then creates the largest sea,

please help me see who I need to be.

I cherish thy who I believe in,

with your magic and my strength I shall win.

Love and passion flows through my veins,

you stopped me from hurting you vanished the pain.

Faith and hope within my soul,

a gift of life you gave I hunger more.

Treasures from the enchanted land,

are solid enough to hold in the palm of my human hand.

Mother Goddess in the sky above,

wraps around me and shows me true love.

Bless your gentle heart I love you,

guiding my eyes I see a dream come true.

Nothing I Fear

My heart is strong it shall never break,
I will hold on no matter how long it takes.
I can survive another day
because I know you'll be there,
I'll speak to you what I must say
because I know you'll care,
Beautiful soul I love you so you're my heart,
my arms wrap around you I won't let go
never shall our bodies part.
I forgot the pain because of you,
you're not the same in all you do.
What can't I see, when I look inside?
What do you want me to be, in order to never hide?
I lay in bed and try to sleep
and your face does appear,
your love I'll keep
because there's nothing I fear.
I'm so happy to the point I cry
you gave that to me,
it's all real
it's not a lie I love you only.

Unforgettable

And that was something I only wanted to need,
but some things aren't mean to be.
So where do I stand in this place?
Why don't I want to remember your face?
It's hard to believe, but I try to go along,
I focus on others who say they're strong.
Because maybe I could learn about their own way;
maybe I'll think twice next time on what to say.
How do I reach the top without falling?
I stop to listen just in case you might be calling.
It's been so long since I've heard from you,
I try to deny everything that is true.
You used to mean everything to me,
but then you left me to be nothing but lonely.
The light wasn't bright enough to really shine,
and towards the end we ran out of time.
All I wanted was to be unforgettable
so that you would always remember me,
but that was before I saw the difference
between what I want and what I need.
Was all that too much for you?
Maybe next time the right thing you'll think to do.

For Loving You

You could care less about me
when it comes to any concern,
a simple letter you couldn't return.
I'm the one fighting to keep in touch,
while you' re blowing me off
you act as if keeping contact is too much.
But I got news for you
just hear me out,
if I feel that you're not listening
then I will shout.
I want to know why you don't acknowledge me?
You were the last person I'd ever expect
to be the kind who'd deceive.
Whatever really happened for it to be this way?
Was it something I didn't say?
I can't sit around guessing all kinds of answers
because you need to help me,
only you know what you need.
I tried to give you everything
and I thought it had shown,
so why do I feel alone?
It's all because of you,

because your love never once came through,
I needed you
but you gave up on me and walked away,
I hate myself for loving you so
but the feelings continue to stay.

Good Thunder

The community of Good Thunder
let me tell you about that small town,
the people make a living by bringing others down.
I lived there for ten years of my life
and it felt like it would never end,
in the school no one was capable of being a friend.
Since I was born in Monterey, California
they acted as if I wasn't human
and they treated me wrong,
they'd tell me things like
"go away because you don't belong."
My family and I got harassed and judged
every waking moment each day,
soon enough I built up the feeling
of wanting to run away.
The people were never decent
I don't think they even know how to be,
they thought that they were better then everyone
especially when it came to me.
The teachers were worse then the students
when it came to calling names,
I was a target to their sick games.

Finally when we moved
I felt like I was waking up from a nightmare
that felt like it would always last,
but soon after that all has happened
I forgot about them all so fast.
I tell myself that I'll never go back there,
it's sad how they never learned how to care.
I don't have one good memory from that place,
from this day on their negative energy I continue to erase.
Those people will never be happy
if they still think their better then all,
they're headed for a lonely life
that will cause them to fall.
I still don't understand
why they always tried bringing me down,
but that's how outsiders are treated
in the small Good Thunder town.

Want to Consider

Exactly how much more clear and professional
would you like me to sound?
You could've responded in a mature manner
without the intentions of bringing me down.
But no, instead you treated me
like I didn't know what I was going about,
the best of luck you say with nothing but doubt.
I would apologize but I did nothing wrong,
you seem to be the only one
who doesn't know what's going on.
Because the less you pay attention
the more you won't know,
if you say it politely
then maybe I'll let it go.
So maybe next time you'll think twice,
you might want to consider being a little more nice.
Now did I sound more clear and professional enough for you?
In addition I was mature about this too.

Because of You

My dearest love I miss your touch,

I love you so very much.

I'm so happy that we've lasted this long,

for our love I will stay strong.

There's so much that you gave to me,

in your arms forever is where I'll be.

You showed me so much that I have never known,

your endless affection has always shown.

What did I do, to ever really deserve someone like you?

Your eyes tell me that you are for real,

your embrace is all I can feel.

Standing beside you I feel so confident,

I seem to get lost in every moment.

I no longer need to dream

because it all has come true,

my reason to be happy is because of you.

I can't wait until the future comes by,

because I know it will always be

just you and I.

www.ingramcontent.com/pod-product-compliance
Lightning Source LLC
Chambersburg PA
CBHW071528120626

46550CB00006B/2386